ONE LIVES, ONE DIES

SRI CHINMOY

One Lives, One Dies
Sri Chinmoy

THE GOLDEN SHORE

The Golden Shore Verlagsges.mbH
Austraße 74, D-90429 Nürnberg, Germany
www.goldenshore.de

Original reprinted as part of special
"Sri Chinmoy Originals" edition
Copyright © 1974 Sri Chinmoy
www.srichinmoy.org
Copyright © 2018 Sri Chinmoy Centre
www.srichinmoycentre.org

ISBN: 978-3-89532-415-4

TABLE OF CONTENTS

PREFACE

In this volume of stories, the Indian spiritual Master Sri Chinmoy lucidly reveals many aspects of the relationship between Master and disciple. He creates in each story a living world in which the reader can readily experience the Master's unconditional love and the disciple's evolving aspiration.

Here Sri Chinmoy answers searching questions about the death of a devoted young disciple, the way to please one's Master and become close to him, the special concern of a Master for his black disciples.

AFFECTION FROM THE MASTER
OR THE DISCIPLES?

"Master, why am I unhappy? I pray and meditate every day, and I listen to you always, yet I am unhappy."

"Son, you pray and meditate every day, but you do not do it soulfully. You listen to me, but you do not do it cheerfully."

"Master, one of the reasons for my unhappiness I am embarrassed to tell you."

"Son, don't feel embarrassed. If you don't give me your embarrassment, how will your embarrassment be perfected and illumined?"

"Then I shall tell you, Master. You know, there was a time when I cried and cried to become your dearest disciple. Now that I have become your dearest disciple, I feel that others should appreciate and admire me. But alas, instead of appreciating me, they hate me. I know they are all jealous of me."

"Sanjit, make up your mind. Do you want my affection and love, or do you want appreciation and admiration from the world?"

"Master, undoubtedly I want your affection and your love. But Master, would it not be even better if I could get striking appreciation and admiration from my brother and sister disciples as well?"

"You are a fool, Sanjit. There is no disciple who would not like to be my dearest disciple. But, at the same time, there are at least a few hundred disciples who will not care for others' appreciation and admiration as long as they get constant love and affection from me. You are my dearest, and you want my constant love, affection and concern; but at the same time you want appreciation from the outer world."

Sanjit felt miserable. He said, "Master, forgive me. I shall never bring up this matter again."

"Sanjit, my dearest son, it is true that one likes to be appreciated and liked by all, both by the Master and by the disciples. But I tell you, if I were asked by someone whether I would like to be appreciated and admired by a wise man or by two hundred fools, immediately I would say that I would prefer to be appreciated and admired by one wise man. Then, if I were asked whether I would like to be appreciated and adored both by the wise man *and* by the two hundred fools, immediately I would say, 'No, no! I want to be appreciated only by the wise man, and not by the fools.' When a wise man appreciates you, his strength enters into you as a solid, dynamic force. The appreciation of the fools is also a kind of strength, but this strength is ignorance-strength. When a fool appreciates and adores you, his ignorance-strength enters into you as a heavy, lethargic force. So I tell you, I will never care for the appreciation and admiration of fools.

"Also, very often appreciation and adoration from others, even from brother and sister disciples, is not sincere at all. They may flatter you just so that they can become closer to me on your recommendation. Many times it has happened that spiritual Masters have made others close to them when their dearest ones have shown considerable fondness for them. Then these disciples adopted foul means and in many undivine ways they pushed the dearest ones aside. Now who is the fool? Your stupid hunger for appreciation and admiration from all and sundry just enables others to catch and devour you. If you care for appreciation from ignorant people, you have to feel that you are virtually embracing a snake or a tiger.

"But among disciples who are not as close to me as you are, there may be some who are not jealous of you, but who want to imitate you because they feel that you are meditating well, or that you are serving me well, or that in some way you are pleasing me most powerfully. If they try to imitate you, that is not bad at all. They imitate you, not out of jealousy, but out of their own necessity for inner progress. If a disciple who has not been meditating at all in the morning knows that you meditate every morning at five o'clock, then if he also begins to meditate at that hour—not to compete with you or to take you away from me, but just to feed his hunger to become good and divine like you—then he is doing absolutely the right thing. The Master needs many, many divine soldiers who will fight against the undivine forces. One instrument is not enough.

"If you, on your part, show affection, concern and love to others—not out of a sense of superiority, but out of a sincere feeling for the members of your own spiritual family—then I assure you that you will have no cause for worries and anxieties. Your sincere feeling of oneness with them will make you infinitely stronger than you are now. The sincerity of your oneness with your spiritual brothers and sisters will make you a true captain of my divine army.

"But if you cry for appreciation and admiration from others and you do not get it, then you just weaken yourself. And if they give you insincere appreciation and admiration, then their jealousy-arrows will enter into you and weaken you. If you are really wise and divine, then you will say, 'It matters not who is closest to the Master, or whether that person is appreciated by others; all that matters is whether the Master's will is fulfilled on earth. If you can develop that kind of devoted, surrendered attitude to the Master's dispensation, then the Master will eternally claim you as his dearest, best and most perfect disciple. So, my dear Sanjit, have I made it clear to you?"

Sanjit bowed down to his Master with folded hands and said, "Master, make of me your absolutely surrendered disciple. I know I will get the greatest joy only by becoming your unconditionally surrendered disciple, and not by becoming your best disciple."

The Master said, "You are a fool, my Sanjit. The absolutely surrendered disciple will eternally remain my best disciple. If you become my absolutely unconditionally surrendered disciple, automatically you will become by far my best disciple. There can be no difference between my best disciple and my most unconditionally surrendered disciple. In order to become an unconditionally surrendered disciple, always put your Master's need first and foremost in your life, and always take your Master's need as the only need for yourself and for all."

February 6, 1974

My duty is to love God.
God's necessity is to love me.
It is God's Grace that makes my duty
*   successful.*
It is God's Concern that makes His necessity
*   fruitful.*

KHADAL'S DAUGHTER

"Master, I know that I am not pleasing you, but I am helpless. You want surrender from me. I have made my own surrender to you, but where somebody else is involved I cannot surrender to you. You have been asking me to bring my son and daughter, who are fifteen and sixteen, and to encourage them to follow your path. Now, I am an adult. I have gone through life and I have come to the point where I can make my own decisions. But my son and daughter are still very young. I feel that they should wait until they become more mature and then be allowed to make a choice of their own. They may not care to enter into the spiritual life at all. And even if they choose to do so, it is they who should decide whether to accept your path or somebody else's path."

"Khadal, stop your philosophy. Don't fool yourself by telling me that you have made your own surrender complete. You have not made even a fraction of surrender. I tell you, the freedom that you want to give your son and daughter will simply ruin them. Tell me, you fool, when they were young children, did you wait for them to ask you before you gave them milk or curd or anything else? Did you wait for them to make the selection? Did you give them any freedom? You yourself felt that milk would be nourishing, so you gave them milk. Anything that you felt would be healthy for them to eat you gave them. There are things that you gave your son and daughter to eat during their childhood which they eat even now; and again, there are things which they no longer eat now. Similarly, if you give them our path now and they become dissatisfied with it later in life, they can go to some other path. But they need some kind of spiritual food now. For you not to bring them to our path is an unpardonable spiritual crime. It is like refusing to feed your children anything because they are too young to make their own choice."

"Master, please don't be angry with me. Tomorrow I will bring my son and daughter. But I wish to tell you that I am doing this out of fear, and not out of love for you."

"In that case, I don't need your son and daughter. Let them stay at home. Let them wait until you inspire them to come to me or to some other Master. If you cannot bring them to me soulfully and devotedly right now, then I do not need them. But you have entered into the spiritual life and you are following our path. Naturally I, your spiritual father, am feeding you inwardly. I am sure you like my food, for otherwise you would not have stayed with me for such a long time. Tell me, why do you yourself pray and meditate?"

"I pray and meditate for various reasons, but the main reason is because I feel that I am quite old. I am fifty-nine, and since I do not have much time left on earth, I feel the best thing will be for me to get spiritual Peace, Light and Bliss as soon as possible."

"So you know the importance of time?"

"Master, who does not know the importance of time?"

"Then why don't you allow your son and daughter to come and meditate here with me?"

"But Master, they are quite young. Let them mature, and then they can choose their own path. Oh Master, forgive me. Tomorrow I will bring them."

"I don't want them. Since I can't make you surrender to me spiritually, I don't want your son and daughter. You are a self-ish man. You want to eat my spiritual food all by yourself."

"No, Master, never, never! I just thought that since I have gone through ordinary life, vital life, I am now ready for the spiritual path, whereas they are not yet ready."

"You fool! Just because you had to walk along a dark, dirty road, just because you have passed through darkness, do you think that each and every individual has to experience night? No, your son and daughter are innocent. Since the world has not yet captured them, they will run much faster than you. Outwardly you will say that you are not jealous of them, but I definitely know that you would be jealous of their inner progress if they came to me. And another thing I shall tell you: you are a clever man. You want to realise God as soon as possible because you feel that you will soon die. But how do you know that your children will have long lives? They may die before you."

Khadal burst into tears. "Master, Master, don't curse me! Your prophecy always proves true. I don't want to see my dear son and daughter die before I do. That would be simply unbearable. Master, I shall bring them tomorrow and place them at your feet."

"All right, let us see."

The following day Khadal brought his son and daughter to the Master. The daughter, Niti, was full of joy when she saw the Master. She immediately said to him, "How I wish to be your disciple, Master! Please make me your disciple. I will devote my whole life to pleasing you."

But her brother told her father, right in front of the Master, "Father, I don't want to come to this man anymore. He may be your Master, but right now I have no interest in the spiritual life whatsoever. Let me go home." So Khadal's son left the Master and went home.

In three short years Niti made the fastest spiritual progress. She became her Master's dearest disciple, and he was extremely proud of her. One day she went with her girlfriends to the sea. She did not know how to swim, alas, and on that day the sea was very rough. The powerful, tumultuous surges swept her away and drowned her in spite of her friends' greatest efforts to rescue her.

Niti's mother had never cared for the spiritual life. On hearing of her daughter's death, she was so deeply shocked and grieved that she went to her husband's Master and insulted him mercilessly. "Look!" she cried, "this is your protection, this is your spirituality."

The Master said, "I am more sorry than you are about Niti's death. Of course, you won't believe this."

But Niti's mother would not listen. Instead, she accused him and threatened him, saying, "I hate you, I hate you! I have lost my only daughter because of you! I shall do something really harmful to you."

As his wife ran out of the house Khadal said to his Master, "Master, don't worry. She has lost her only daughter, and she has become insane with grief. Soon, by your grace, she will be all right. But I wish to tell you something, Master. You imposed spirituality on my daughter. If she had not accepted the spiritual life, she would still be on earth today, like my son. So you see, Master, what happens when you impose something on others."

"Khadal, I fully sympathise with your sorrow, for your daughter was extremely close to my heart and soul. But if you have really accepted the spiritual life, as you claim to have done, then tell me which is more desirable: to live on earth indefinitely in an unaspiring, animal way or to live a shorter but higher and more fulfilling life, leaving earth when God's Hour strikes?"

"Master, this is not the time for me to answer your philosophical questions. My loss is my loss, after all. I feel miserable. True, I will not allow my wife to harm you in any way; but today, like my wife, I am also deeply grieved. I don't know who will console me or how we will console each other. I do not know how we can ever be consoled."

"I know this is not the time for me to offer you my supreme philosophy, but once and for all I wish to tell you that I knew perfectly well that your daughter had only a short life ahead of her. That is why I insisted that she meditate with me and become my disciple. In three years' time the progress that Niti made soared far beyond my imagination. In three short years she far surpassed you. When we leave the body God does not ask us how many years we stayed on earth. He wants us to show Him our spiritual progress, divine progress, inner progress, which is the only progress that is necessary in this world. Your son may stay on earth for many, many years, and you may stay on earth and enjoy life for a number of years, but your progress—not to speak of the progress of your undivine son—will never equal your daughter's progress. It is not how many years you stay on earth, but how fast you progress that is of paramount importance. The Christ stayed on earth for only thirty-three years. But look what he achieved during those thirty-three years. You have been on earth for sixty-two years and look what you have achieved!"

"But Master, how can you compare me with the saviour Christ?"

"Khadal, I do not see anything wrong with that. Like you, Christ was also a son of God; but look how fast he realised the Truth. We are all children of God. Like the

Christ, we too will one day be able to say unmistakably that we and our Father are one. Had your daughter stayed on earth without accepting our path, perhaps she would have lived a little longer, but she would not have made any significant progress. In your outer eyes Niti's death is a supreme loss. But in my inner eye and in God's Vision, she is the supreme glory of God. You will see that a life of enjoyment is not and cannot be a life of satisfaction. It is only a spiritual life, an inner life, that can give us abiding satisfaction.

"If it is God's Will that someone accomplish a specific task and he succeeds in accomplishing it, then it is foolishness for that person to stay on earth any longer. The destined hour of departure depends on the individual. At times the Supreme wants an individual to realise something and then give his achievement to the world at large. But in some cases the Supreme says, 'I want you to accomplish only this much in this incarnation and then continue your achievement in your next incarnation.' The Supreme wants these aspirants to go back to the world of rest and return to earth at some later time with the same Peace, Light, Bliss and divine capacities in order to make further progress. There is no hard and fast rule. But it is useless to stay on earth without making any progress. There are many, many people who stay on earth for well over a hundred years, but they are living a useless life, an absolutely useless life. But again, if it is God's Will, one can live a long life in order to give one's aspiration and dedication to Mother Earth."

"Master, I understand your philosophy, but don't you have a father's heart, a mother's heart? We are missing our dearest daughter so badly. Our hearts are broken to pieces. She was our only daughter. This is not the time for me to apply your philosophy in my life."

"I fully realise that, but you gave me the impression that you had accepted the spiritual life wholeheartedly, and that you had surrendered to me in everything. If you had really surrendered, you would not have suffered so much today because you would have felt that it was God's Will that your daughter died today.

"Son, identify yourself with Heaven and earth at once. Feel that as Mother Earth you are mourning the loss of your daughter, and that as Father Heaven you are rejoicing over the glorious arrival of your daughter. Here on earth you are suffering because you have lost your daughter; there in Heaven you are rejoicing because you have gained back your daughter. Now that she has gone back to Heaven, naturally you are sorry; but is it hard for you to believe that when your daughter entered into the earth-consciousness, her dear ones in Heaven also felt sorry?

"Here we are constantly playing the game of hide-and-seek. First we hide in the earth-consciousness, and seek in the Heaven-consciousness, and then vice versa. So you see, if you are really one with earth and Heaven you should feel that before your daughter was on your right hand, and now she has gone to your left hand. Death and life are like two neighbours. You stay with one neighbour for one week, and then the following week you stay with the other neighbour. You don't feel miserable about going from one to the other."

"Master, your philosophy is correct; I don't deny it. But after all, it is my loss."

"All right, you may think it is your loss. But I take it as my gain that what I could not give you in twenty years I was able to give Niti in three years. You are not pleasing me and you are not pleasing Mother Earth. Niti's passing may be your loss, but it is my gain and the gain of the Supreme, for your daughter has gone to the other world to please the Supreme in His own Way."

February 6, 1974

THE DEATH
OF GOROKSHA'S MASTER

There was once a spiritual Master who
was seventy-five years old. He was suffering from a very serious heart condition.
Goroksha, one of the intimate disciples who
had tremendous love for him, became very
alarmed. Goroksha called in many eminent
doctors, but the doctors could not cure his
Master. Day by day the Master's condition
worsened. Finally, with a heavy heart,
Goroksha went to a great occultist in order
to find out whether his Master would long
survive or whether his death was immi-
nent.

The occultist, who happened to be a family friend, was extremely kind to Goroksha.
He asked Goroksha about his wife and children, and Goroksha gave him all the news
about them. The occultist was pleased with
Goroksha and said, "Look here, I shall write
down on a piece of paper exactly when your
Master is going to die. There, now I have
written the exact date, but I am sealing it in
this envelope. It is entirely up to you to de-

cide what to do with this envelope. If you open the envelope and see that your Master will live for a long time, then you will be very happy. On the other hand, if you see that your Master is going to live for only a few days, then because of your extreme sorrow you will be of no further use to your Master during the brief remainder of his stay on earth. But if, out of fear of losing your Master very soon, or out of a smug feeling that your Master will not die for another twenty or thirty years, you one day have the inclination simply to discard the envelope, I tell you, on that very day you yourself will die."

One month passed and Goroksha did not open the envelope, nor did his Master die. Then Goroksha had a dream. In the dream he saw that his Master had died. His whole being was thrown into a sea of grief, and he became senseless. The next morning, even when he saw that his Master was still alive, his whole body continued trembling with uncontrollable fear. He felt that on that very day his Master was going to leave the body, so he told his family that he intended to discard the envelope. They immediately protested, "How can you do that? If you discard the envelope, you will die today."

"That is what I want to do," he replied. "I don't want to see my Master's death."

Goroksha's wife pleaded with him. "Master is an old man," she said. "Even if he dies today, he has played his role. But you are only fifty years old. You should stay on earth for a long time to do Master's work."

"After Master's passing, what joy will I have in life? If I will never see his beloved face again, what beauty will there be to appreciate on earth?" said Goroksha. "Other people can do Master's work as well as I. I don't want to stay on earth after his death. There will be nothing for me to live for."

"But you know that for a great spiritual Master, the inner world and the outer world are the same," said Goroksha's son. "He does not have to stay on earth physically in order to guide us; his spiritual light and power will guide us even after he leaves the body."

"True," said Goroksha, "even when he leaves the physical body, he will continue guiding everyone as he does now. But I wish to say that I won't be able to bear the loss of my Master. I strongly feel that Master will die soon, either today or tomorrow, and so the best thing will be for me to discard the envelope and die."

Again Goroksha's wife, daughter and son vehemently protested, but he was adamant. He tore the envelope into shreds and discarded it. And lo and behold, Goroksha got an immediate heart attack and died then and there.

When the Master learned of his dearest disciple's death and of his dealings with the occultist from Goroksha's grief-stricken family, he felt miserable. He said to himself, "I never knew, I never even suspected that my Goroksha was a rogue. I thought that he would work for me in my physical absence. Such a clever fellow! He has deserted me. Now I won't be able to punish him here in this world, but I *can* enter the other world and send him back to earth again." With that, using his occult power, the Master left the body and entered into the higher worlds in search of his dear disciple.

While he was travelling through the vital world in eager quest of Goroksha, the denizens of that world asked the Master, "Are you really entering into the soul's world with the idea of sending your dearest disciple back to earth to work for you and propagate your views, or are you going there because you badly missed your dearest spiritual son on earth?"

The Master gave a broad smile to the denizens of the vital world and said, "It is up to you to decide."

February 6, 1974

BE CAREFUL OF EX-DISCIPLES

"Master, I am at times so puzzled and so confused."

"Why, my son?"

"Master, when some of your disciples leave you, they create such problems for me."

"What kind of problems do they create?"

"They cause unnecessary confusion."

"Do you mean that you also lose faith in me?"

"No, never!"

"Do you mean that they have a sound and convincing justification for their actions?"

"No, never!"

"Then why are you confused?"

"I do not exactly know why I am confused. But what frightens me, or what confuses me, rather, is this: if I speak to them or mix with them, you may throw me out of your ashram. Recently some of my very close friends left you. Now please tell me, what kind of relationship shall I maintain with them? Shall I totally ignore them? Shall I mix with them? Shall I try to bring them back?"

"Son, wait and see what they do. It is usually not good to ignore anybody. But if necessity demands, you can be totally indifferent. Whether you mix with them or not entirely depends on their inner life. Once someone leaves my ashram, it is useless to try and bring him back. It is just like the case of a broken mirror. You can repair it, but it can never be made perfect again.

"No matter who leaves a Master's ashram, he will usually speak ill of the Master. When a disciple who is still with the Master hears an ex-disciple's critical remarks, he may become a victim to doubt; and doubt is nothing but poison in the spiritual life. There are a few reasons why someone may leave my ashram: either he loses faith in me, or he is jealous of others' achievements and closeness to me, or he wants to go back to his vital pleasure-life. But I tell you, by re-entering into the vital pleasure-life, he cannot discover his true self; by being jealous of others, he cannot discover his true self; by losing faith in me, he cannot discover his true self.

"Now I wish to tell you what you should do when a person leaves our ashram, whether he is a personal friend or a mere acquaintance. If an individual leaves our ashram and immediately goes to some other Master, you should not get angry with that disciple. You should always remember that, according to my philosophy, it is quite immaterial which Master takes a seeker to God. What is of paramount importance is whether the seeker actually reaches God. You can talk to someone who has left our ashram and accepted another Master if necessity demands. But do not go out of your way to mix with him, either to bring him back or to convince him that he has done something really wrong. You can, however, inwardly pray to the Supreme a few times to grant him illumination so that he will be able to know whether what he is doing is right or wrong. But if you mix with him often, you will only enter into a terrible conflict and meet with real spiritual disaster.

"Again, if you see that after having left our ashram, someone feels that he can go his own way, that he does not need any Master now that he has taken all the help he needed from me, you can be kind and sympathetic to him. You may feel sorry that since the poor fellow is no longer taking the help of his Master, who was his private tutor, his spiritual journey will take a very long time. But in no way should you try to convince him that he has done something terrible. If you do so, you will again only enter into unnecessary conflict, and this conflict will illumine neither of you. Still, if you feel the inclination to do so, you can pray to the Supreme a few times for his illumination, so that he will always be able to do the right thing.

"But if someone leaves me and speaks ill of me, of all my disciples, of God; if he mercilessly criticises the whole spiritual world; if he himself does not meditate but wants to take away some of my other disciples, then you have to know that his case is simply hopeless. He is really a sick man, and if you associate with a sick man, you yourself are apt to fall sick. You are certain to be affected by this spiritual disease. Spiritual life is for the sincere man, and not for the fool. If your heart wants to go and help him, you will only be caught by his ignorance. You will be of no help to him at all! So I tell my disciples not to mix at all with an ex-disciple who is bitterly against the spiritual life, against God, against me, against other spiritual Masters and everything that is spiritual. So, my son, when someone leaves our ashram, try to see which category he falls into, and then deal with him accordingly."

"Master, after hearing this from you, on the one hand I am so illumined, but on the other hand I am totally disgusted with the stupidity of these disciples. No matter why your disciples leave you, they are simply stupid; they are simply sick. I will have nothing to do with a stupid or a sick fellow. But again, my own stupidity and sickness have not yet left me totally; otherwise, I would not have asked you this question. Who cares who comes and goes, as long as you give me eternal shelter at your feet, as long as I can grow inside your heart and fulfil you in your own way. I know and I strongly feel that if someone has seen you even once, he is forever yours. Outwardly he may leave you, but although his heart's aspiration may be eclipsed from time to time, he will eventually look inward again to see the illumining sun which is your universal Self, and which ever illumines and ever fulfils the searching, seeking and crying humanity."

The Master blessed the disciple with deepest joy and pride and said, "Son, you have understood my philosophy. Now manifest my philosophy in the life of your soul's illumination, the life of your heart's aspiration and the life of your body's dedication."

February 6, 1974

Life

An ordinary life plays with ignorance.
A religious life plays with rites and
*   ceremonies.*
A spiritual life plays with the inner
*   planes of consciousness.*
A divinely transformed life will play
*   with the consciousness of Immortality.*

MY CHOSEN CHILDREN

There was a spiritual Master who had a few hundred disciples. Among them there were quite a few black disciples. The Master was exceedingly fortunate in that his black disciples and his white disciples were on very good terms. Both black and white found a safe and perfect home in their Master's heart.

But one day a white disciple came to the Master and said, "Master, I am extremely sorry to have to ask you this. Believe me, Master, I have tremendous love for my black brothers, but there is one thing I do not understand. Why do you call them your chosen children? In which way are they superior to us? I tell you, Master, it is not jealousy that is making me miserable; it is just my curiosity to know in what sense they are superior. If you tell me why they are superior, I shall be extremely grateful to you and, at the same time, infinitely more proud of my black brothers than I am now."

"Son," replied the Master, "since you are calling my black disciples your brothers, I am ready to illumine you. You say that it is not out of jealousy that you are asking me why I call my black disciples my chosen children. Well, I believe you; but if you are telling me a lie, if you have a clever motive behind your question, then God will have to forgive you.

"You know that I am your spiritual father. Inside me there are two lungs functioning perfectly. I also have two eyes that see well. Now, I consider my white disciples and my black disciples as two lungs or two eyes. When both lungs and both eyes function well, I feel I am healthy, sound, normal and perfect. But if one of my lungs or one of my eyes does not function well, I shall feel miserable.

"My black disciples and my white disciples are equally important, but I call the black disciples my chosen children—not because they have surpassed the whites, but because they have my special concern, for they are now doing something which they either have not tried to do or have not been given the chance to do before.

"Suppose there are two sons in a family. The older son is seven years old and the younger is one year old. The older son knows how to walk and how to run, but the younger one still crawls. At times he tries so hard to stand up and equal the capacities of his older brother. When the parents see the great and sincere effort the little one makes, their joy knows no bounds. The older one went through the same stage when he was a little baby, and the parents got the same joy from him when he made an attempt to stand up and walk. The parents always encourage their little one to stand up and walk, and when they see that he is standing they are extremely delighted. They feel that their little one has really accomplished something. When the older brother sees that the younger brother has learned how to walk, he does not become jealous. On the contrary, just because his brother is younger, he, like his parents, tries to help his brother and gets tremendous joy from his brother's accomplishment.

"The blacks have started their spiritual journey a little later than the whites. In a family we cannot say that just because the little one has started walking a few years later, he is inferior. I am fully justified in calling both my white disciples and my black disciples my true spiritual children. There is no competition in our spiritual family, only oneness. The manifestation of oneness is God-perfection in unity's multiplicity. Here there is no question of inferiority or superiority. In our family we need only the feeling of oneness. We have to know that everything is a matter of time. God's destined Hour strikes for each and every individual at a specific time. When the little one, the newcomer in the family, accomplishes something, the parents say that he is going to be most brilliant, best in every way, and that he will surpass everyone. This encouragement of the parents is not insincere; it is their strong feeling and their lofty hope. Today's hope grows into tomorrow's reality. The parents cherished the same kind of hope for their older son when he was a little child, and this hope also became a reality.

"Again, I call my black disciples my chosen children because the Supreme in me has chosen them out of countless black people. Furthermore, the Supreme in me tells me that my black disciples will play the role of pioneers. They will bring their vast community to the Supreme in me—their spiritual father—and to the Supreme in themselves. They will act like older brothers in the family. At God's choice Hour they will lead and guide their younger brothers to the Supreme. That is why I call them my chosen children."

"Master, you said that if I had any clever motive for asking you this question, God would forgive me. Master, is there anybody who can deceive you? I was jealous, but I wanted to conquer my jealousy. Your compassion makes us feel at times that you do not want to see through our tricks; so we venture to ask you things which we would otherwise never dare to ask. Master, not only have you illumined my mind totally today, but also you have given me a new heart, a heart of vastness wherein I can sing the song of oneness. Black and white are inseparably united in their effort to realise the Highest in the heart of the Master and to manifest the Highest in the heart of every aspiring soul on earth."

February 6, 1974

Freedom

Real freedom does not depend
  on the world around us.
Real freedom depends on our acceptance
  of God's Will as our very own.

ONE LIVES, ONE DIES

Once there were two brothers who had been disciples of an occultist for a number of years. They were extremely devoted to the occultist and helped him financially and in many other ways to run his ashram. The occultist was extremely fond of them, too.

Each brother had a son. Alas, it happened that one day both sons were attacked by cholera, and it was only a few hours before death would claim them. The brothers ran to their Master's ashram and knelt and wept at the Master's feet, begging him to save their sons.

The Master said to the elder brother, "Don't waste time. Since your son's case is serious, go and take him to the hospital." The elder brother immediately ran home and took his son to the hospital. To the younger brother the occultist said, "You don't have to take your son to the hospital. Take this blessing flower and place it on your son's head. It will do what is necessary."

In six hours' time the son of the elder brother died in the hospital. But in fourteen hours the younger brother's son was completely cured. Now it seemed that, in the same family, one son had been saved by the Master and the other had simply been allowed to die. Happiness and sorrow reigned together in the family.

The two brothers were very, very close. Despite his grief, the elder brother was happy that his nephew was safe. And the younger brother and his wife both felt miserable over the loss of their nephew. A sea of joy and a sea of sorrow were wrestling with each other.

The following day the elder brother went to the Master weeping bitterly and said, "Master, you did not care for my son. You asked me to take him to the hospital, but the doctors could not cure him, and he died. Both my younger brother and I are so close to you, but you cured his son and not mine. I am not mean. I am glad that you have been kind enough to save at least one son in our family. For that I am grateful. In my nephew I will feel my son's presence, for my nephew is extremely dear to me and I have always thought of him as my own second son. But Master, if you had saved my son, too, I would have been so happy and delighted to get back both my sons from the jaws of death. Master, would you mind telling me why you did not save my son? But if you don't want to say, don't say, Master. I surrender to your will."

The occultist said, "I saw occultly that the time had come for your son to die. What was I to do? When I saw that his death was destined, I asked you to take him to the hospital for medical treatment. I knew that, if he could get the best medical treatment, you would be able to console yourself and your wife. If I had given your son a flower, as I gave your nephew a flower, then your wife, who has not accepted my path, would immediately have sneered at the flower. If your son had not died, your wife would have said, 'Nonsense, it was not the occultist who saved my son.' And if your son *had* died, as he did die, she would have insulted you and scolded you, and said, 'Why didn't you send my son to the hospital, you heartless rogue?' Since your wife has not accepted my path, I am in a difficult position. You are a dear, devoted disciple of mine, and I know that you understand and believe what I am saying. But your wife does not understand my philosophy at all. If your son had lived, she would have given the credit to God. Now, I would have been happy if she had given credit to God. For me it is quite immaterial whether she believes in my power or not, because the little capacity I have came from God. But if your son had died, your wife would have been furious, and she would have insulted both of us for this kind of treatment with the flower. So it was for your sake that I had to ask you to take your son to the hospital. I did all this so that she could not blame you or me."

"True, Master, my wife would have accused me if our son had died without medical treatment, but you did not give me the opportunity to have faith in your miracle-power. You could have given the same kind of flower to my son and cured him."

"My child, it is not a matter of faith. It is true that faith cures, but this was something predestined. God had selected the hour for your son to leave the world. Since it was ordained by God, I could not change your son's fate, no matter what kind of faith you had in me. In your nephew's case, even if I had not given him a flower, he would have been cured. He did not take any medicine and he did not go to the hospital, but he was cured, because it was destined that he would survive."

Now while the Master and the disciple were having this serious conversation, the disciple's wife came in quite unexpectedly and started insulting the occultist, saying, "You unkind, cruel creature! My husband has given you thousands and thousands of rupees, just as his brother has done. How is it that you have cured our nephew but not our son?"

At this, the husband buried his head in his hands in utter shame and said to his wife, "For God's sake, leave this place, and do not speak to my Master in that way. He is my Master, he is my All."

The wife became furious. "He is your all! Come home today, and I will show you who is your all!" Then she threw a volley of insults at the Master and cried, "Tell me, do you really have occult power? If you do, how is it that you saved one son in our family and not both?"

The husband himself became furious and said, "You must not talk to my Master in such a contemptuous manner! He is my Lord, he is my All."

"Do you mean that the way you are my lord, and my all, in that way he is also your lord and your all ?"

"I am not your lord and I am not your all. God is your Lord, God is your All. My Master is my Lord and he is my All."

"So you have rejected me today in front of this unkind, cruel man!"

The occultist burst into laughter and said, "What can you expect, Shiva? He is now with an unkind man, so naturally he will act like an unkind man. His misbehaviour is all due to the bad company he keeps."

The husband said to the occultist, "Master, I shall always cherish this bad company. I want to stay with you always. Now I have no son. This wife of mine who does not accept you I have tolerated for many years, but now I am convinced that she will never accept you, so I will not go back home. From now on, I shall stay here with you, and I shall serve you."

"Impossible!" said the wife. "God made us one. No human being can separate us. Your Master is, after all, a human being."

The Master said, "Poor Shiva, I am not preventing you from taking your husband home. He is your all and you have every right to take him back home with you."

The disciple said, "Master, for God's sake, for my sake, please do not torture me. I am not her all. But if ever she accepts you, you will be her all. Right now, since she is not accepting you as her Master, I place her at the Feet of God. God is her All, and He will take care of her. Master, you are my God, you are my Lord, you are my All."

Suddenly Shiva realised what was about to happen in her family, and she fell at the feet of the Master and said, "Is there any way I can get my husband back? I have lost my only son. Now I am losing my husband, too. Please tell me, is there any way I can get my husband back?"

The Master said, "I do not know. I have no way to console you."

The husband said, "Yes, I know a way. Shiva, you have touched my Master's feet. Now pray to him with folded hands and say that you also want to be his disciple. If you accept him as your very own, if you claim him as your all the way I claim him as my all, then I shall go back home with you."

"You cannot make this kind of demand," said the Master. "I will never force anybody to become my disciple. If somebody loves me, if he sees and feels something divine in me, only then do I accept that person as my disciple. If you force her to accept me, I will not be able to accept her."

The disciple said, "Master, it is entirely up to you whether to accept or reject her."

Shiva said to the occultist, "Master, I am accepting you, not because my husband has threatened me, but because I am seeing something in you and I am feeling something in you which I have never seen or felt before in my life."

The Master blessed her and said, "Shiva, my daughter, I shall give you a supreme boon. Your nephew will become my very close disciple. He will be at my feet throughout his life. Your son, who left us yesterday, will always be inside my heart. His body has left us, but his soul remains within my heart." The Master asked Shiva and her husband to look at his heart. He then used his occult power and showed them the living face of their son inside his heart.

Both husband and wife touched their Master's feet with boundless gratitude. Shiva said, "You are not only our Master, but our Lord and God. To see our son inside your heart is more than consolation; it is a true, unmistakable revelation of what God, through the Master, can do for the disciple."

The Master said, "Again I tell you, your nephew will be always at my feet. He will work for me, for my manifestation in the outer world. Your son will work for me inwardly, in my heart, silently inspiring me, devotedly helping me to fulfil my role here on earth. Alas, we human beings unnecessarily blame God's dispensation."

Shiva said, "Do not include yourself in that statement, Master. It was we unfortunate disciples who doubted God and who doubted you. But Master, the nights of doubt are all gone. From now on we shall grow and glow in the effulgence of your eternal midday sun."

February 6, 1974

THE THIEF

"Master, you always need money. Today I have come up with an excellent idea."

"What is it, my son?"

"Master, I shall be able to make you really rich."

"How, my son?"

"Master, among your disciples it seems I am the one with the most money. Please do me a favour. Whenever I give you money, please let me know what you used it for. If you let me know how you used my money, I shall give you double the amount."

Then the Master said, "That is an excellent idea, son. But since you are so nice to me, instead, I shall tell you what I am going to use your money for in advance. Not only that, but I shall actually show you how I am using your money."

"Oh Master, I have all faith in you. It is not necessary to tell me in advance or to actually show me how you are using my money."

"Oh Sukhen, I am all love for you. Therefore I want to make you feel that I am a real stranger to deception."

"Master, deception is not meant for you; it is only meant for a mortal like me. Anyway, please take this hundred-dollar bill from me. I am placing it at your feet."

The Master said, "Thank you, my dear Sukhen. Now this is how I am going to use your money. Tomorrow morning I will give this hundred dollars to the first person I see when I open my door."

Sukhen said, "It is an excellent idea, Master. And as soon as I know that you have given the money away, I shall give you two hundred dollars." The Master gave Sukhen a broad smile.

Early the next morning when the Master opened his door, lo and behold, there he saw his dear disciple, Sukhen, meditating with folded hands. The Master gave the hundred-dollar bill to Sukhen and blessed him as well. Sukhen was deeply moved and gave the Master an offering of two hundred dollars. Then the Master said, "Sukhen, I will tell you how I am going to utilise this money. Tomorrow morning I am going to give the money to whoever calls me first on the phone."

"Master, I am not an early riser. With greatest difficulty I got up today. So someone else will get the two hundred dollars tomorrow. But when you tell me that you have given the money to that person, then I will give you four hundred dollars."

The following day, early in the morning, the Master got his first call from a little girl. And this girl was none other than Sukhen's little daughter, Kaga. "Master," she said, "I have a severe headache. Please tell me whether I should go to school."

"You don't have to go to school," replied the Master. "Come here instead. I am your inner school and inner teacher. I shall give you a very good lesson."

Kaga ran over to the Master's house very happily in spite of her headache. He gave her a toy, a box of candy and a glass of milk. Then he gave her an envelope and said, "Don't open it here. Take it home and open it in front of your parents. There is magic inside it."

Sukhen's daughter was so thrilled to hear the word magic that she literally grabbed the envelope and ran home. On reaching home she cried aloud, "Mommy, Daddy, the Master has given me magic! Come and see it!"

The mother and father came to her immediately, and with boundless joy, enthusiasm and curiosity the little girl opened the envelope. Lo and behold, inside it were two one-hundred-dollar bills. She held them up in front of her parents and said, "Two hundred dollars. It is all for me! It is all for me!"

"Kaga," the mother said, "indeed this is

all your money. But since you told us that you had a severe headache this morning, please lie down and go to sleep. When you get up, I will give you your money back."

When little Kaga went to sleep, the mother went to a toy store and bought a package of play money. She put the play money inside the envelope the Master had given Kaga, and removed the real two hundred dollars. In the meantime, Sukhen went to the Master's house and gave him four hundred-dollar bills.

The Master gave him a broad smile and said, "Now I will tell you how I am going to use this money. Tonight, I shall ask all my disciples to come to my house for a special meditation from one o'clock to six o'clock in the morning. Whoever keeps his eyes wide open during the meditation and does not once close his eyes will get the four hundred dollars as a prize from me."

All forty of the Master's disciples came to meditate. For about two hours all the disciples meditated well, with their eyes open. But alas, at the end of two hours everybody felt tired and exhausted and one by one they began closing their eyes—everyone, that is, except Sukhen's wife, Nihar.

At six o'clock the Master chanted *Aum* and all the disciples woke up. "I am so glad that all of you have come back to this world," said the Master. "We need you badly in this world to manifest the Supreme, and I was so afraid you might never return."

Then the Master said, "Nihar, you alone have stayed awake. Here is my gift." And he gave her the four hundred-dollar bills. Everybody was very surprised to see so much money for that kind of meditation. Some of the disciples were very poor, and inwardly they cursed themselves, thinking that if they had known what the Master's gift was to be, then they, too, could easily have kept their eyes open for five hours. But outwardly they all congratulated Nihar. The Master blessed Nihar from the depth of his heart and then blessed all the returning travelers from the other world. They all felt a little bit sad, not because they had not gotten the prize, but because they had made friends with the sleep-world when they were supposed to be doing good meditation.

After everybody left, Sukhen gave the Master eight hundred-dollar bills. The Master then said, "Tomorrow I shall invite all the disciples to come and meditate with me early in the morning, and at that time I will show you how I am going to use these eight hundred dollars."

Sukhen said, "That is fine, Master. But up until now you have told me in advance how you were going to use the money. Why is it that you are not telling me this time?"

"Why such curiosity, Sukhen? Was it not you who told me that I did not have to tell you ahead of time how I was going to use the money? Now it is your curiosity which wants to know. Have you descended, Sukhen? Has your consciousness fallen?"

"No, Master, I have not yet descended. Tomorrow morning I will come and see how you use the money."

The following day all of the Master's disciples came to his house to meditate. They meditated for about an hour, and everybody had a good meditation. Then the Master said, "In the spiritual life, the most important thing is obedience. I need and expect obedience from each of you. Now I want to see who can fulfil my request first."

Everybody immediately cried out, "I can! I can!" Sukhen's voice was the loudest.

The Master continued, "I shall be eternally pleased with and give a most coveted gift to the disciple who will come up to me now and give me a smart slap."

Everybody was embarrassed and shocked. "Master, what kind of request is that?" they asked. "We don't need your gift. For God's sake, please keep your gift. We do not want it."

But Sukhen stood up and said, "Master, I

do not know what your gift will be. It is not because of the gift that I am going to give you a slap, but because I want to be your most obedient disciple. That is why I am obeying your command." With that, Sukhen went up to the Master and gave him a smart slap.

The poor Master began to cry like a child. Immediately the other disciples rushed over to Sukhen and thrashed him mercilessly. In spite of his pain the Master pleaded with his disciples not to thrash Sukhen: "After all, Sukhen has fulfilled my request." But despite the Master's pleas, the disciples beat Sukhen to within an inch of his life. Then, at the Master's request, they took him to a hospital.

In two days Sukhen was well enough to return home. The Master went to visit him immediately. He said, "My Sukhen, punishment from you I deserve because it was for executing my wish that you got this severe beating. I pleaded with your brother and sister disciples not to strike you, but they did not listen to me."

Sukhen quietly accepted the Master's apology, but his heart was burning for revenge. He said to the Master, "It seems to me, Master, that you really need thousands of dollars to run your spiritual community. Since I have lots of money and a large heart,

I will lend you a large sum without any interest. And someday, when you get a lot of other money from the rest of your disciples, you can return the money to me. But, Master, there is only one thing. Since it is a very large sum, I wish to give it to you privately."

The Master was a little surprised at Sukhen's new offer, but he accepted it, saying, "This evening, before I start my meditation, you can come and give me what you want to give."

That evening Sukhen went and placed before the Master one million dollars in cash. Then he said, "Master, may I remain here while you meditate?"

"Certainly," said the Master.

"But Master, sometimes you go into a trance and stay there for two or three hours. During that time I may lose all patience. Will I be excused, then, if I leave the money here in front of you and go? Will it be safe?"

The Master said, "Certainly, my son. Nobody is here, only you and me."

The Master started meditating, and in a few minutes, went into a very deep trance. Sukhen observed the Master's trance for about twenty minutes. Then he quietly opened the bundle of money and took out two hundred-dollar bills, which he placed at the Master's feet. The rest of the money he put back inside his shirt and, after prostrating himself before the Master, slowly and quietly he left the Master's house and went home.

Since he was very rich, Sukhen had three phones in his house. When he got home he told his wife that he had just come from the Master's house, and that he had never before seen the Master in such a high trance. Even though the Master had not invited anyone to come and meditate with him, Sukhen asked his wife to inform their brother and sister disciples that they should go and secretly watch. He himself informed some disciples to go and see the Master's unprecedented trance. He even had little Kaga tell some disciples.

The Master was still deep in trance when everyone arrived to see him. They were all observing soulfully and devotedly, with folded hands, when Sukhen and his family came. They were the last to arrive. After a few seconds, Sukhen gave a loud, piercing cry. Everyone was shocked, and insulted him in angry whispers. "How dare you interrupt Master's trance!" they hissed. "Just wait! When the Master enters into his normal consciousness again, we shall thrash you as we did the other day!"

But Sukhen said, "We shall see thrashes whom. Right now I am going to call the police. You are a bunch of thieves. When I saw the Master, I placed at his feet one million dollars. The Master is my witness. He will bear me out and support me in my accusations. Now I see only two hundred dollars there. When Master comes out of his trance, the police will give you a nice lesson."

Fifteen minutes later the Master came out of his trance and was surprised to find that so many angry-looking disciples were gathered around him. Sukhen was positively emitting fire through his eyes. "What is wrong with you, Sukhen?" asked the Master. "Why are you all so upset?"

"Master, I tell you that all your disciples are thieves and rogues. They have stolen all your money. Look, Master, only two hundred dollars remain. Master, you always taught us to be generous. Out of my love for them, I wanted to share with them my highest delight when I saw you in your transcendental consciousness, so when I went home, my wife, my daughter and I informed them about your unprecedented trance, which I had never seen before. Now you see, Master, what they have done. Out of your one million dollars, only two hundred dollars are left."

The Master quietly asked which disciple had come first. Immediately Vinu stood up and said, "Master, I came first but I did not see any money. I only looked at your face and drank in the nectar of your eyes."

"Who came second?" the Master asked. Shibu stood up and said, "Master, I came in second but I did not see any money. When I came in, I saw Vinu praying to you very devotedly and soulfully. So I started praying to be granted the same kind of devotion that Vinu had, so that I could receive abundant Peace, Light and Bliss from you."

"Who came in third?" the Master enquired. Tartu stood up. "I came third, but to be very frank with you, Master, when I came in I saw only two hundred-dollar bills."

The Master then said to Vinu and Shibu, "What am I going to do with you two? Tell me, have you really stolen my money?"

They immediately shed bitter tears. "Master, you have realised God. You are our all. You can easily read our hearts. If you feel that we have stolen the money, Master, then do anything you want with our lives."

The Master went deep within and after a few seconds said to Sukhen, "What am I going to do, my son?"

"You don't have to do anything, Master. I am going to do everything for you. I am going to call the police. Forgive me, Master, it is not my money now; it is all your money. But I tell you, Master, in a few minutes the police will be able to get all the money back from these thief-disciples of yours."

The Master went deep within once more and then gave Sukhen a meaningful smile. "I am helpless," he said. "What can I do?"

Sukhen phoned the police, and told them his story. A few minutes later three police detectives came in. They said to the Master, "You have a good reputation, sir. How is it that you have kept such thieves and rogues in your ashram?"

The Master replied, "Who is a thief and who is a rogue? Who is a gentleman and who is an honest man? How am I going to know unless and until I observe their conduct? It is a disgrace that you should have to come here to catch a thief, but God has promised to me that the thief will be caught by you. With your broad experience, you will easily be able to detect the real thief." Sukhen jumped with joy.

The detectives asked the two suspects, "Have you left here at all since you first arrived to see the Master's trance?"

"No, sir, we have gone nowhere. We have been here the whole time," Shibu replied.

"Who was the third person to arrive this evening?" asked the policeman.

"I was," said Tartu. "I was the third person to come to see the Master's trance, and I saw them both here when I arrived."

"Have you any idea how long before your arrival these two suspects were in the presence of the Master?" they asked.

Tartu replied, "It was a matter of only a few moments. I was not many steps behind Shibu."

Then the detectives enquired how the others had come in. They said that they had all come in within a few seconds of each other.

The Master said to the police, "I leave everything up to you. My disciples are supposed to be sincere. Since the real culprit will not tell me who he is, it is beneath my dignity to stay here. You may do anything you want with the suspects. I am going to retire upstairs."

The police searched the two suspects thoroughly, and then they searched all the other disciples, including Sukhen. Finally they said to Sukhen, "This is very strange, but we must try to do something for you. Do you think we could come to your house to ask you a few questions about these two friends of yours, privately? If we can come to your house and ask a few questions about them, I am sure we will be able to recover your Master's money."

Sukhen, his wife, his daughter and the police detectives all went to Sukhen's house. Lo and behold, to the wide astonishment of the police, there was a big, heavy wallet on the kitchen table. Immediately one of the detectives grabbed it and began counting the money inside. The other two policemen joined him. They counted it once and then they counted it twice and each time found that the sum was just two hundred dollars less than a million dollars. Without any further words, the policemen took the money and went to the Master's house.

Sukhen shouted and screamed, "Police, police! You are thieves! You are taking away all my money!" But the police just laughed and laughed.

All the disciples were still wondering and suffering over the loss of the money when the policemen arrived with the good news. On hearing the happy noise of the disciples' voices, the Master came downstairs. When they told him who the actual thief was, he said simply, "I knew it, I knew it."

The arrival of three more policemen, called by Sukhen to recover his money from the first three, added a touch of pure chaos to the scene of happy confusion.

Everyone laughed and laughed when the whole story was explained. Then the Master said, "I don't blame anybody. I take the full blame upon myself because it was I who was first tempted to accept money from Sukhen. Temptation ends in frustration, frustration ends in destruction. But destruction is finally illumined by God's Compassion."

February 8, 1974

Peace

Peace is fulfilled Delight.
Where peace is, the light of Delight has
replaced the right of ignorance-night.

MONEY-POWER
AND CONCERN-POWER

There was once a spiritual Master who had about sixty disciples. Even though most of the disciples were poor, every Monday they used to give a love-offering of money to their Master. Now it happened that on a certain Monday it was raining very heavily, and only three disciples came to the meeting in the Master's house.

The three disciples, who were all women, inwardly felt happy that they alone had been brave enough to come out in the heavy downpour. But outwardly they expressed sadness that there was not a good turnout. The Master, as usual, gave a most significant discourse. At the end, he told the three disciples, "I am glad that you have come. But even if nobody had come, still I would have given my discourse. The four walls, the door, the windows and the ceiling would have been my silent and grateful audience. Sometimes I feel that my disciples do not pay any attention to my talks anyway. They whisper and squirm during my speech and cough and clear their throats just to make noise. But my silence audience—the walls, door, windows and ceiling—has always shown me love and veneration."

"But Master, your silent audience cannot manifest your divinity," said one of the women. "It is we who can and will manifest your divinity."

"I am not so sure," said the Master. "No doubt you can manifest my divinity, but I am not so sure that you will."

Then the Master asked the three disciples to come up to him one by one for blessings. After he blessed the first disciple, Rekha, she said to him, "You do so much for me, for my inner life, for my soul. I have been giving you only one dollar a week as my love-offering. In spite of my best intentions, I cannot give you more. I am sorry that I am so poor." The Master gave her a soulful smile.

Then it was Shikha's turn. After being blessed by the Master, she gave him a twenty-dollar bill and said, "Master, I am so happy that today I am able to give you twenty dollars. Usually I am only able to give ten dollars."

The Master asked, "Are you only happy, or are you proud as well?"

Shikha said, "Master, I am a bit proud, too." The Master gave her a sad smile.

Finally the Master blessed the third disciple, whose name was Lekha. After being blessed, Lekha gave the Master two hundred-dollar bills and said, "Master, I am so sorry, but even though I give you two hundred dollars every week, this money is not unconditionally given. Something within me wants to know, out of curiosity, what you do with my money, and I feel really miserable for that. Master, forgive me." The Master gave Lekha a compassionate smile.

Then Rekha said to the Master, "Master, will it ever be possible for me to give you more than one dollar a week? How I wish to give you ten dollars a week! I know you need money badly to run your spiritual mission. You have a few disciples who can afford to give you lots of money, but they think that you don't really need any more money. Each one thinks that since everyone else gives, he can be excused. After all, they think, the Master is not starving."

"My daughter, it is not how much you give me but how devotedly and how soulfully you give that is of paramount importance."

"I know that, Master, but if I could give you more money with the same kind of devotion, would it not be more useful for your divine manifestation?"

"That is true," said the Master, "but I

wish to tell you that it is always advisable to be happy with what you have, and cheerful in giving the Master what you can afford to give devotedly and unconditionally."

Next Shikha said to the Master, "Master, you always tell us to be happy so that we can make faster progress, and I always try to be happy. I have given you twenty dollars with happiness. I am sorry I allowed a little pride to enter me, but since I gave you two divine things—money, which you can utilise for your Centre, and my happiness—can you not forgive my one undivine thing, my pride?"

The Master said, "If you give me even nine divine things and one undivine thing, I shall feel sorry and miserable. To get one undivine thing is to get a drop of poison, which can ruin the entire contents of a vessel of nectar. Because of your pride, I have given you a sad smile. I could have been totally indifferent to you, to your pride and your money-power, but my forgiveness wanted to illumine your ignorance."

The Master then said to the third disciple, Lekha, "Lekha, I am really proud of your sincerity. You want to know how you can be unconditional when you give me money. You have no pride. You are all sincerity. You have no cleverness, no tricks. Now I will tell you how you can give me money unconditionally. The moment you give me money, please feel that you have dropped your money while walking along the street. You have lost the money, and you have no idea who has found it."

"But Master, if I have that kind of feeling, then I will feel sorry for a while."

"You are right. You will be sorry for a while, but then you will forget about the loss, since you can do nothing about it. But, my dear Lekha, there is an even more effective way. Please feel that I am a multimillionaire, that I really do not need your money. Please feel that by giving this two hundred dollars every week, you are in no way helping me. Please feel that I do not need your money, but you give me the money because you get a sense of satisfaction. You get a sense of satisfaction that God has made you a chosen instrument to manifest the divinity that your Master embodies. If you feel this, you will be grateful to the Master for using your money to manifest the Divine on earth. When you consciously exercise your humility-power, you will easily be able to offer your money-power unconditionally to please me and to fulfil my divinity on earth."

Lekha said to the Master, "I have given you my money-power, and in return you have given me the power of liberation from the world of ignorance."

Shikha said to the Master, "I have given you my pride-power, and in return you have given me forgiveness-power, which is the only power that can save and illumine my life."

Rekha said to the Master, "I have given you my incapacity-power, and in return you have given me your love-power and oneness-power. Master, your oneness-power has made my life a garland of gratitude, and this garland I place at your feet for your constant use."

The Master said to the three disciples, "My daughters, since you three have pleased me most satisfactorily according to your own standards, your own levels of consciousness, I am offering to each of you my most precious Concern-power. Take it from me according to your receptivity-capacity."

February 8, 1974

THE MASTER
WITH THREE NEWCOMERS

There was once a good and kind spiritual Master. One day, when his disciples had gathered around him and he was about to start meditating, a young man came running up to him. "Master, Master," he cried, "I wish to become your disciple."

The Master said, "Now we are about to meditate. Sit down and meditate with us. Afterwards I shall speak to you."

"Oh Master, please tell me one thing," the young man said. "Please tell me, when you leave the body can I become the spiritual head of this community? I wish to become your disciple only on the condition that you make me the leader of your spiritual community in your physical absence and when you leave the body."

Everybody was shocked. The Master said, "What about the person who has been the leader of my community for such a long time? And what about those who have helped me establish a strong spiritual community? Should they not be the leaders of my ashram in my physical absence?"

"Master, true, they have helped you immensely in founding the spiritual community. But I wish to tell you that since they are not God-realised souls as I am, they won't be able to run your spiritual community as well as I. You and I are both God-realised souls. You have to admit it." The Master gave him a meaningful smile, and the young man continued, "Master, since you are old, you will be leaving the body very soon. However, I am quite young, and I feel that in your absence I will be able to run your community much better than anyone else."

All the disciples laughed and laughed, but there were a few who would have been inwardly very happy if the Master had actually accepted this fellow as the head of his ashram, for they were jealous of the present leader of the community. Even though this young man seemed like such a silly fellow, they felt that anyone was preferable to their president. But outwardly everyone showed contempt and extreme disrespect for the young man.

The Master said, "Now don't waste our time any longer. Come and meditate with us. I will see what we can do for you after our meditation."

"Oh Master, there is another reason that I came here," the young man said. "For the

64

last few months I have had a terrible stomach pain. Every day I have been suffering. So I came to ask you to kindly touch my stomach and cure my pain. First you must cure my stomach pain and then you can make me the leader of your centre. On this condition I will gladly become your disciple."

One of the Master's disciples said, "If you are a God-realised person, why do you need our Master's help? Why don't you use your own occult power to cure yourself?"

The young man said, "I am sorry, but I have come here to speak to my friend. I am a spiritual Master and he is a spiritual Master, so we are on the same level. It is beneath my dignity to speak to you people."

The Master said, "All right, since one God-realised soul needs the help of another God-realised soul, let me bless this young man," and he placed his hand on the young man's head.

"Why are you touching my head?" asked the young man. "My head is perfectly all right. It is only my stomach that is bothering me. So please touch my stomach if you want to cure my pain."

The Master said, "I don't have to touch your stomach. If I touch your head and bless you I will be able to cure you."

But the young man replied, "Is it beneath

your dignity to touch my stomach? Is only my head divine, and not my stomach?"

The Master said, "Everything of yours is divine, but your head is your highest part. When you offer your highest part with humility to someone, then the Force acts most powerfully. I am bringing down Peace and Light from above to cure you. You have to be respectful and devoted to the higher Peace and higher Light that I am bringing down. That is why I want to bless your head. If you don't want me to touch your head, then you can leave this place."

The young man said, "All right, let me meditate with you and see if my stomach condition becomes better."

"And after we meditate," the Master said, "I will see if I can do anything about making you the head of my centre or of a newly formed centre, which I shall invite new seekers to join."

The disciples then said, "Master, you won't have to work hard for that. We shall go out and bring disciples according to his standard. He is a fool, and we will bring him all the fools of the world. He will have no trouble establishing a centre."

The young man became furious. "You are cutting jokes with a God-realised soul!" he shouted.

The disciples responded, "If you are a

God-realised soul, then why do you have to come here and beg our Master to let you run his mission in his absence? Why don't you open your own ashram? And why do you have to cry to our Master about your stomach problem? Go to a doctor or cure yourself!"

The young man said, "I am going to meditate with you here, and at the end of the meditation your Master will say that I am going to take his place when he leaves the body."

The Master said, "All right, O great Yogi, God-realised soul, but please let us start to meditate."

Just as they began to meditate another young man rushed in. "Master, Master, I would like to be your disciple," he said. The Master asked him to sit and join the group, but the young man kept speaking. "Please tell me the exact day that I am going to realise God." The Master said he didn't know. "You do not know? Then what kind of Master are you? You claim to be a God-realised soul, and a God-realised soul certainly knows when another person is going to realise God."

The Master said, "You will realise God at God's choice Hour."

"But you don't know when God's choice Hour will dawn for me. So what kind of inseparable oneness do you have with God? I am not going to be your disciple."

The other disciples immediately cried out, "Who wants you to be our Master's disciple? Who needs you? Get out of here!"

"I won't get out," he said. "I am telling you the right thing. He who has realised God knows everything. So your Master must know when, sometime in the near future, I am going to realise God. He is refusing to tell out of mere jealousy."

Everybody laughed and laughed, and the Master, with a smile, said, "Well, since I am too jealous to tell you when you are going to realise God, then you had better go to some other Master. He will surely tell you." But the young man refused to leave. Finally the Master said, "All right, I shall tell you about your future, but first I shall tell you about your immediate past and your present. I will tell you only a few incidents about your past life. What you did a few years ago, what you did just yesterday." The man immediately jumped up and started to run away. The Master said, "No, no! Don't run away! Just come and meditate with me, and I will tell you about your God-realisation. Only first I will tell what you did yesterday and what kind of life you are leading now." But the man did not return, and the Master laughingly exclaimed, "Rascal, rascal, rascal!"

Again the Master and his disciples were about to meditate, when a third man came in. "I see you are about to meditate," he said. "Master, please forgive me, but I wish to ask you something. I wish to be your disciple."

The Master replied, "Then come and meditate with us. After the meditation, I will let you know whether I can accept you as my disciple."

But the man said, "Master, first of all you have to know whether I accept you or not. I will accept you only if you make me your dearest disciple. I can serve you in so many ways. I have thousands and thousands of rupees. I also have a big family and all the members of my family will be at your service. My wife is a very good cook and she will cook most delicious meals for you. My father is a great lawyer, and he will be able to help you if you have any legal problems. My mother is a famous singer, so she will sing for you and bring other famous people to you. Furthermore, I have three sons and three daughters who are all grown up. They, too, will serve you in every way. So I will help your mission in hundreds of ways if you make me your dearest disciple."

The Master said, "I tell you, hundreds of ways I do not want. All ways are good, but for me the most important way is to give me your heart. If you can give me your heart, I do not need money, I do not need all kinds of material capacities. I need only the disciples' hearts. If I receive your heart I will be able to manifest all other qualities in and through it."

The man said, "Impossible! Just from the heart you will be able to make everybody a good disciple?"

"Yes. And my best disciple need not be one who will be well-organized or have earthly capacities and material possessions. No! A person who has won the admiration of the world need not be my greatest disciple. My greatest disciple will be the one who is devoted to me wholeheartedly, the one who makes unconditional surrender to me. That person can have earthly name and fame also, but what really matters to me is his heart, his love, his humility, his devotion, his surrender."

The man said, "Well, I have all of those good qualities. Just give me a chance. Just tell me that you will make me your dearest disciple, and I will give you money, devoted service, love, everything."

"First do the things that you have said and then I will make you my dearest disciple," the Master declared.

"Oh, you want me to give you all my money, and then you will kick me out. You won't recognise me at all."

The Master replied, "Do you think that I am a fool? If I don't get your service, your spiritual wealth, then why should I make you my dearest disciple? Again and again I keep telling you, it is not the material wealth that can make someone my dearest disciple. My dearest disciple will be the person whose life is dedicated at every moment only to serving me, pleasing me, fulfilling me, manifesting me unconditionally."

"I can take up the challenge," the man said. "The only thing is, I am afraid that you will not keep your promise. When I do everything for you, you will still be partial and still keep closest to you the person whom you have already accepted as your dearest disciple."

The Master said, "If you don't believe me, then how am I going to believe you? The world depends on the strength of mutual belief. You don't believe me and I don't believe you. So let us remain in the world of unbelief and disbelief. But please allow me to meditate. I have already been interrupted three times today so now I wish to tell you either to sit down and meditate with us or to go home."

The young man said, "I have come here to examine you and to examine your disciples.

I tell you, the world is not going to accept you because you are not accepting me, the right person, to be your dearest disciple."

The Master said, "If I accept you as my dearest disciple, what will happen to the one who is already my dearest disciple?"

"Oh, that is no problem. If I become your dearest disciple, I can make that person my dearest disciple."

This was too much. The person who was the Master's dearest disciple came up and said, "For God's sake, shut up or get out of here! I am the Master's dearest disciple and I tell you, if you want to be the dearest disciple of someone, then be my dearest disciple. I won't ask anything of you. Just let us meditate, and I will make you my dearest disciple without fail."

The intruder got furious and said, "Is this what your Master has taught you—this kind of callousness and stupidity? I have so many good qualities to give to the world, but what do you have? Nothing! The only thing that you have is the fact that the Master has made you his dearest disciple."

"Yes," the Master said. "I made him my dearest and I will keep him my dearest. My dearest disciple is whomever I make the dearest, not whoever thinks he deserves to be dearest. Everybody may feel that he is dearest to the Master. If a disciple feels that he is the nearest and dearest in the inner world, then naturally that person will make the greatest progress. But if someone claims that he should be the leader or that he should be the closest to the Master because he has many more good qualities than the ones who now hold these positions, he is sadly mistaken. In all cases it is the Master who makes the choice for his own reasons. Finally, why does the Master make someone his dearest disciple? He makes him his dearest disciple either because he has made unconditional surrender to the Master or because his surrender far surpasses the surrender made by others."

All the three intruders received a real lesson from the spiritual Master that day.

February 9, 1974

The Guru

A real Guru is the selfless, dedicated and eternal beggar who begs omnipotence and omnipresence from God to feed his unconsciously hungry and consciously aspiring disciples, in perfect conformity with their souls' needs.

THE MASTER
WITH HIS EIGHTEEN DISCIPLES

The Master with His
Six Unsatisfactory Disciples

"Master, are you pleased with me?"
"Sorry, I am not."
"Master, why not?"
"Because your sincerity is lip-deep."

"Master, are you pleased with me?"
"Sorry, I am not."
"Master, why not?"
"Because you feel that the highest spirituality and the lowest animal sensuality can go perfectly well together."

"Master, are you pleased with me?"
"Sorry, I am not."
"Master, why not?"
"Because you don't see the inner world and the outer world as one whole. Because you don't see the outer world through the eyes of the inner world."

"Master, are you pleased with me?"

"Sorry, I am not."

"Master, why not?"

"Because you think that you have given me everything. But I want to tell you that you have given me next to nothing. You have given me thirty percent of your sincerity, ten percent of your dedication, forty percent of your concern, fifty percent of your aspiration, hardly one percent of your outer success and none of your inner success."

"Master, are you pleased with me?"

"Sorry, I am not."

"Master, why not?"

"Because you think that my mission is my mental hallucination, my conscious fabrication, my deliberate imposition and my self-aggrandisement. You think that I use the terms 'God's Mission' and 'God's Manifestation on earth' just to acquire boundless name and fame for myself. You feel that there is a yawning gulf between me and the Supreme. You feel that there is no God in me—only the constant dance of ego."

"Master, are you pleased with me?"

"Sorry, I am not."

"Master, why not?"

"Because you are extremely happy that,

although you are not of me, you are totally for me. Do not cherish this false idea. Unless you have become totally of me, you can never be really for me.

"Dear children, I wish to tell you that it is the human in me that is displeased with you, and not the divine in me. The divine in me is inseparably one with your imperfections, limitations, bondage and ignorance."

The Master with His Four Characterless Disciples

"You are a characterless fellow, am I correct?"
"Master, you are absolutely correct. Now Master, just because I am characterless, I have come to you to learn how to turn over a new leaf."

"You are a characterless fellow, am I correct?"
"Master, you are absolutely correct. But Master, forgive me. Right now I am not consciously aware of my wrong actions. But even if I have not done anything blame-worthy, on the strength of my oneness with the members of my spiritual family, I

am sure that I have done many deplorable things. Therefore, Master, in all sincerity and humility I wish to say that you are perfectly right in your assessment of my life: that I am a characterless fellow."

"You are a characterless fellow, am I correct?"

"Master, you are absolutely correct. Master, I beg to be excused. Since it is beyond my capacity to recollect what I have done wrong—or let me say, *if* I have ever done anything wrong—I want to prove to the world that my Master is always right. How? Just by doing something undivine today, I shall prove that my Master's statement is ever faultless."

"You are a characterless fellow, am I correct?"

"No, Master, you are absolutely wrong Never was I characterless; nor am I now, nor shall I ever be in the near or distant future. I hate you because you have exposed me falsely to the wide world. From now on I shall have to hide my face and my life. But my mouth will vehemently stand against your realisation, revelation and manifestation on earth. Your embodied spirituality is my life's only curse. Dear sir, you are absolutely wrong."

The Master with His
Four Faithless Disciples

"Master, forgive me. I have lost all faith in you."

"My child, why?"

"I thought you would give me much outer success."

"My child, I am the wrong person. Please go to some other Master."

"Master, forgive me. I have lost all faith in you."

"My child, why?"

"I thought you would bring much harmony, peace, joy and understanding into my family."

"My child, I am the wrong person. Please go to some other Master."

"Master, forgive me. I have lost all faith in you."

"My child, why?"

"I thought you would give me true aspiration."

"My child, in order to get pure and genuine aspiration, you have to sell yourself unconditionally—body, vital, mind, heart and soul—to the divine in me."

"Master, forgive me. I have lost all faith in you."

"My child, why?"

"Master, you have not given me realisation."

"My child, I am more than eager to grant you realisation. But first you have to grow into the eternally climbing flame of aspiration. And then you have to stay in my boat. If you do not jump out of the boat and enter into the sea of ignorance any more, at God's chosen Hour I shall grant you the highest realisation. And I wish to tell you that it is my ever-descending divine Compassion which expedites God's chosen Hour for you and which is the very breath of God's chosen Hour in you. Love me. Lo, the Supreme has come into your life of love. Devote yourself to me. Lo, the Supreme is offering you His choicest Blessings. Surrender yourself unconditionally to me. Lo, the Supreme is eternally yours, the eternal Servant of your unconditional love, devotion and surrender."

The Master with His
Four Advanced Disciples

"I am proud to tell you that you are an advanced disciple of mine."

"Master, I am so glad to hear that. That is what I longed for."

"I am proud to tell you that you are an advanced disciple of mine."

"At long last my aspiration is bearing fruit. Master, I am really happy to hear it."

"I am proud to tell you that you are an advanced disciple of mine."

"My sacrifice and your concern have made all this possible, Master. I am extremely happy."

"I am proud to tell you that you are an advanced disciple of mine."

"Master, I offer my heart's tearful gratitude for your kindest blessingful honour. Master, I offer you my long-sought realisation. Your name is infinite and eternal Compassion, and my name is Immortality's aspiring life and ascending breath."

ABOUT SRI CHINMOY

Sri Chinmoy is an internationally renowned spiritual leader, who dedicated his life to promoting world harmony and international understanding. Through his teaching of meditation, his music, art and writings, his athletics and his own life of dedicated service to humanity, he tried to offer ways of finding inner fulfillment.

He was born in East Bengal, India (now Bangladesh) in 1931. When orphaned at the age of 12, he entered the Sri Aurobindo Ashram in southern India, where he prayed and meditated several hours a day, having many deep inner experiences. He also took an active part in ashram life and was decathlete champion for several years. It was here that he first began writing poetry to convey his widening mystical vision. He remained in the ashram for 20 years, deepening and expanding his realisation. Following an inner command Sri Chinmoy went to America in 1964, to share his inner wealth with sincere seekers.

After coming to the United States in 1964, Sri Chinmoy continued his literary activities – eventually completing thousands of poems, essays and questions and answers, as well as large numbers of paintings, drawings and songs. His poetry touches upon virtually every aspect of the spiritual journey – from struggles and wonderments of the young pilgrim to the ecstatic realisations of the illumined Master. His prose is equally encompassing – focusing on man's relationship with God, global peace, worlds beyond the mind and the vast universe within. Viewed as a whole, his writings offer a unique, deeply spiritual, luminous world view.

Sri Chinmoy's creative output grew out of his work as a teacher and man of peace.

During the years he lived in the West, he opened more than 350 meditation centres worldwide and served as spiritual guide to multitudes of students. He advocated "the path of the heart" as the simplest way to make rapid spiritual progress. By meditating on the spiritual heart, he was teaching, the seeker can discover his own inner treasures of peace, joy, light and love. The role of a spiritual Master, according to Sri Chinmoy, is to instruct his students in the inner life and elevate their consciousness so that these inner riches can illumine their lives. In return he asked his students to meditate regularly and to nurture the inner qualities he helps them bring to the fore.

Sri Chinmoy was teaching that love is the most direct way for a seeker to approach the Supreme. When a child feels love for his father, it does not matter how great the father is in the world's eye; through his love the child feels only his oneness with his father and his father's possessions. This same approach, applied to the Supreme, permits the seeker to feel that the Supreme and His own Eternity, Infinity and Immortality are the seeker's own.

This philosophy of love, Sri Chinmoy felt, expresses the deepest bond between man and God, who are aspects of the same unified consciousness. In the life-game, man fulfills himself in the Supreme by realising that God is his own highest Self. The Supreme reveals Himself through man, who serves as His instrument for world-transformation and perfection.

Sri Chinmoy personally led an active life, demonstrating most vividly that spirituality is not an escape from the world, but a means of transforming it. He has written over 1,600 books, which include plays, poems, stories, essays, commentaries and answers to questions on spirituality. He has painted thousands of mystical paintings, and his drawings of "soul-birds" number in the millions. He has also composed more than 20,000 devotional songs.

Sri Chinmoy established a wide range of cultural, humanitarian and spiritual programmes. Through these innovative projects, which foster the universal values that underline all great cultures and faiths, he touched the lives of millions of people with his message of peace and love. He offered twice-weekly meditations at the United Nations and gave hundreds of peace concerts in the U.S. and overseas. In addition, he founded the Oneness-

Home Peace-Run, a biennial Olympic-style relay in which runners pass a flaming peace torch from hand to hand as they travel around the globe. He also prompted international good will through his own athletic endeavours, primarily weightlifting, and towards the end of his life worked tirelessly to encourage peace through sports. Sri Chinmoy passed away in 2007 at the age of 76.

More information about the life of Sri Chinmoy, his writings, his music, his activities and about the activities of the Sri Chinmoy Centres worldwide can be found under:

SriChinmoy.org
SriChinmoy.tv
SriChinmoyLibrary.com
SriChinmoyPoetry.com
SrichinmoyArt.com

www.ingramcontent.com/pod-product-compliance
Lightning Source LLC
Chambersburg PA
CBHW070644030426
42337CB00020B/4164